GW00570001

THE WILLIAM POEMS

THE WILLIAM POEMS

Ginny M Meades

The Book Guild Ltd
Sussex, England

First published in Great Britain in 2004 by
The Book Guild Ltd
25 High Street
Lewes, East Sussex
BN7 2LU

Typesetting in Bembo by
MRM Graphics Ltd

Printed and bound by Kyodo Printing Co, Singapore
Under the supervision of MRM Graphics, Winslow, Buckinghamshire

A catalogue record for this book is available from
The British Library.

ISBN 1 85776 847 7

CONTENTS

FOREWORD

Grief is potentially the most creative of human emotions. With pain-filled honesty Ginny, the author of these poems, in her bereavement opens up a seed-bed for such creativity.

When I first read them I felt that I was sharing in a dance of contradictions, where opposites moved powerfully together to weave a pattern of wholeness. Great sadness partnered anger. They in their turn gave place to dawning hope and a beauty remembered. Running through the whole is a stark realism where cynicism finds no place and powerful sentiments stop short of sentimentality.

The threatening shadow of bitterness is dispelled by the growing assurance that 'The painful lot that cuts us deep must needs give way to the gifts we are given to share and keep'. There is no attempt to hide from the recurring sorrow.

The sudden death of a beloved partner finds no comfort in the oft repeated platitude 'Remember the good times'. Yet laughter from the past often resurfaces and together with the fun a reminder of the playfulness of the beloved.

The seeds of hope blossom and Ginny is able to stand apart from 'the sea of pain'. She learns to face the 'little demons' and to recognise that they 'must be knocked down. KNOCK 'EM SIDEWAYS by whatever and which way. For beneath the pain God listens to our cries'.

Canon Peter Spink

TRIBUTE

Eastbourne Herald Friday May 17, 2002

BRIAN MEADES, one of Eastbourne's most popular and charismatic sportsmen, died suddenly last Saturday while on an angling trip in Sardinia.

The Herald has received the following tribute:

Bry bowed out in true Meades' style in Sardinia eight days after his birthday.

He died as he lived, quietly, after a good evening's fishing in the prestigious Hippocampus International Shore Event.

Archives recording his sporting activities run to several volumes and make fascinating reading.

His humour was legendary, a great practical joker with a gift for putting people at ease. Throughout his life he was resolute in his stand against injustice and abuse; he held human dignity in high regard. His integrity was faultless, intact and unshakable. He championed the underdog and the underprivileged.

Brian was a self-employed builder. He was a skilled craftsman who learnt his trade apprenticed to a fine old craftsman. His workmanship going back over the years can still be seen to this day.

One of Eastbourne's finest ever allrounders, Bry's achievements spanning over 50 years kept Eastbourne to the fore literally across the world.

In the '50's he played water polo for Eastbourne and was part of the hugely successful squad of that era.

During that period, together with Dickie Dowle, he kept the much sought after Sussex Lifesaving Award in Eastbourne for a running stretch of some six years, repeatedly trouncing Eastbourne Police Squad.

During his army days he carried off the light heavyweight box-

xi

ing championship of all Egypt against fearsome opposition. Again, good humoured modesty helped him resist army requests to fight professionally under army colours. He was a crack shot. He left the army with a glowing report.

Back in civvies he rowed stroke for Eastbourne with friends Johnny Otto, Clive Willis and Bernie Miller. He was the only outsider ever to beat Emmanuel College at their own game.

Later, he fixed his sights on angling. The angling scene has never been the same since that day! He found himself with the 'old guard' in the early days of EFSA and they loved our boy. Together with his great buddy the legendary Clive Richards, he proved superlative both at sea and on the beach.

During the '70s the pair were unstoppable and with breathtaking displays of sheer skill brought magic to EFSA. Bry holds the greatest number of EFSA's coveted gold pins than any other Englishman.

Still later he also fished for the NFSA and through selection by both organisations travelled the world.

Brian is the only Englishman to hold the King Badouin Medal for sporting achievement. He is the only angler to win the English Beach and Boat Championships in the same year.

Locally he fished for Pevensey Bay Aqua Club where he was also safety officer. He helped to establish this club. Prior to this he fished for the Workers where he worked hard to help get the section off the ground.

He founded the Conoflex Team in the '70's along with matchmen Gary Dunk, Clive Richards and Ron Lambert, also helping form the Sussex Beach League, where they scooped the championship for five years out of seven.

He designed rods, working closely with his long standing friend, Carroll MacManus whose rods today are much sought after. He wrote for various angling papers and featured regularly in the talented Chris Down features

In Sardinia on May 11 Bry bowed out as he had lived—in quiet dignity after a good angling session. This gentle, modest man with the competitive edge simply nodded off as the car transporting his group back pulled into the home straight

With him in Sardinia was his wife Ginny (Moe). The trip to Sardinia was his birthday gift to her and as usual she was with him all the way.

LOVE'S SOFT VOICE

'Come with me.'
Love's soft voice caresses mind.
"I will take you way out there
… and …
You'll leave yourself behind.'

'Come with me.'
Love's soft voice, gentle, kind.
'I will make your dreams come true.
I will show the really you.
… and …
You'll leave your shell behind.'

'Come with me.'
Love's soft voice strokes
the heart and soothes the mind
'Come with me. Leave all behind.
I will show you what is real.
I will show you what is true.
I will give you back your you,
stolen in your earthly climb
we'll leave the nasty all behind.'

I went with love.
I tasted all.
And it is true.
Dimensions new.
You leave the nasty all behind.

1

TEENAGE DREAM

I met him first at sweet sixteen
When in my dream we danced.
I held him in my heart and mind
Through hockey, swimming, exam grind
    And I knew I'd find him
      helped by chance.

Five hundred miles and years ahead
At eighteen I travelled south.
And there at college summer ball
we danced again, ignoring all.
And as we waltzed the hours away
    I knew profound
    My dreamt of husband
    I had found.

From girlhood dream of yesteryear
He'd come again and come to stay.
And I always knew 'twould be that way.
No doubts; misgivings; neither fear
    I knew.
How could a young girl see so far ahead
    So clearly and so right ?
How could it be that once again
We'd re-live our dancing through the night ?

Don't ever say dreams can't come true.
Willie and me are living proof that they just do.

2

DEATH OF WILLIAM

I gazed into his lifeless eyes.
So big. So blue. So beautiful.
My ears ignored my heartbreak cries.
He seemed so fine and wonderful,
So kingly royal. So dignified.
His great frame in repose.
My ears ignored my heartbreak cries
as I gazed in silent awe.

If this is death, the quiet sleep,
what measure is our life?
How dignified my gentle man
slipped quietly from this worldly strife.

I held him soft in long embrace.
I stroked his head. I kissed his face.
My gentle man of measured pace
just slipped away to another place.

And I surrendered to my heartbreak cries.

LURE OF THE SEA

'I'm going down the road,' he'd say.
And off he'd go for quite some time.
For years I'd say, 'Aha. Uhum,'
and turn to other things my mind.

Then one meal-burnt day I asked outright.
'Which road do you go down?'
He looked surprised – amazed in fact –
and laughed away my little frown.

'Just to the beach to see my boat.
Thought you knew, of course.
I wondered why our dinners burnt.
We seem to suffer more than most!'

4

THE LONG DRIVE

The sleek white Cadillac purred quietly down the lane.
The children gazed in rapt delight
      at the beautiful sight
that was to take them to Uncle Bry
      on this his special day.

A tall, kindly man in softest grey
      gestured them inside.
And their little faces turned quite pink
as they stepped aboard, six blue eyes open wide.

We glided behind smoked windows out of sight
      of solemn faces along our route.
And watched with mixed emotions tight
      as we passed close huddled little groups.
The children quietly dived for coke from the shiny mirrored bar.
Dutifully, they tried so very hard
to softly drink with solemn sips the sugared sweetness at their lips.

Along lined avenues, streets and roads
to the rendezvous we went.
Then straight along the seafront, gazing at the sea
he knew and loved so well.

On and on we went, blurred faces peering in.
Resolve was weakening fast
I closed my eyes.
The children chattered; and Comfort came.
Then, eyes opening, I saw at last our solemn destination;
and flowing groups, silent bent, parting like ghosts
as through great gates we went.
Who were they all; and going where?
The car slid to a halt; and as I stepped outside
I realized they'd all come round
to wing my William homeward bound.

ADONIS

Oft at night when in our bed
I'd gaze at his mighty frame.
A Greek Adonis lying there.
So perfect, neatly made.

Myself, a skinny little thing.
Small waist, short legs, big brain.
How came he beautiful as this?
Perfection in a mighty frame.

I'd just be musing on such things
When one blue eye would open wide.
'Go to sleep, you pesky thing.'
And down beneath the sheets I'd slide.

GOLDEN DUST

Like specks of gold dust his ashes twinkled on the
sea.
We drank goodbye, our glasses high.
Fourteen of us, faithful, true,
Like some great knight's retinue.
Watching his golden dust floating by.

Then we tossed our yellow roses to the deep.
They bobbed and danced in reverence sweet.
The boat turned curve.
And from the other side
we watched our roses circle round
the chidren's posy
as if in filial homage bound.

Devoted each, strong and true,
his ever faithful retinue.
We gazed in silence at the circle tight.
And I caught my breath and drove back
the tears that welled inside
at the moving sadness of the sight.

My gentle man; my angling king
was drifting through the waves he loved.
Was sparkling, smiling, twinkling bright
as the rosy sun gave way to night.
All that ocean and beyond;
my man, caressed and held
by the sea he loved.
Exactly as he knew it would ...

Footnote: William's last fishing venue, the night he died.

7

BONDING

Some folks find it hard to understand
why two souls bond for life.
It's as if you feel a special cloak
That envelops both with bright sunlight.
It wraps around, warm and snug
'til both your souls touch tight.
That's how you bond for life.

It's making up a deficit.
It's balancing the two.
It's give and take.
And build and make.
And help and lead.
And rest and do.
Making up a deficit.
And balancing the two.

It's fitting in
and considering.
It's being there for
and administering.
It's caring, sharing.
Protecting, pairing.
And balancing the two.

It's being stronger
than the loner.
It's supplying a demand.
It's also being outright owner
of the best bit in the land.

THAT NIGHT

Relentless rain lashed my nightgowned frame
as, numbed by pain, I stumbled back
      to our room,
whilst William, now white in death,
was taken to the mountains high
      there to lie
until formalities could be done.

I stumbled through the rain-lashed dark,
cutting my leg on jutting rock
      yet feeling naught.
At last I made it to our room.
      I stood alone.
Some merciful numbness held my hand that night
and brought a strange detachment, holding tight
the well of tears that were to stay locked away from others' sight
      as months turned into year.
      No one would see me cry.
      The burden's mine.
      Not theirs to make them weep and sigh.

Room reached, emptiness o'erpowered; transfixed I stood
until detachment gave me first the task that must be done.
Ice cold fingers gathered documents; and neatly stacked.
Little piles of clothes began to grow across the new- mopped
floor.
      William's Ginny's.
      Ginny's. William's.
Each pile matched. One for one. Just as always so.
His with mine. Mine with his.
      Neatly folded.
      Neatly stacked.
The clothes that were not going back.
If his body I had to leave,
so too, a part of me would stay
close, as always was our way.
Through the long dark I worked
'til what was left I lay aside.
His rods; his fishing gear;
my clothes to wear.
Nothing more would I take back.

Daybreak sent me to our bed.
      I crawled inside.
      His half empty.
      My half dead.
I cuddled over, holding tight the pillow white
that held his head before that night .

And I felt an overwhelming pain.
And so bereft. And lost.
I closed my eyes, soft called his name.
I knew my world could never be the same.
I set my face.
Knew my task.
My world I'd have to face.
I had to go back home.
      Alone.

THE FLIGHT BACK

An empty seat.
No hand to hold.
Try not to weep.
Be strong and bold.
Don't dwell upon that room up there
in mountains high
where his body lies
alone and cold.
Be strong and bold.

The plane lifts off; and the urge to leap
is fought and won.
Bite the lip.
Look straight ahead,
not down at disappearing land that holds him dead.
Be bold and strong.

Blank the mind.
Anaesthetise.
Don't read; don't talk; don't close the eyes perchance
the scenes wreck the calm exterior;
and shatter sure the mask.
Hypnotise the self.
Sublimate the shock.
Brace yourself for touchdown task –
and the aftermath
that's surely soon to be your lot.

REMEMBERING

It cuts me deep when I think
of his lonely journey home.
      I weep.
      I weep.
      I weep.

We couldn't meet him.
Couldn't greet him.
And could only wait at home.
      I weep.
      I weep.
      I weep.

How could I let my fine man
know I didn't want to leave him so.
But I had to go. I had to go.
      And I weep.
      I weep.
      I weep.

I would never hurt him.
Couldn't ever hurt him
in our life of many years.
But I had to go.
I had to go.
And I cannot stem the tears.

BETRAYAL

Did I betray him? I ask myself
a thousand times a day.
Should I have stayed and brought him back.
Myself;
and
he; all that way?

Where did my wifely duty lie.
There
or
here?
Which the most – beside his corpse
or
here to make his farewell fine?

My puzzling mind knew not which course
I had to take; which soul-mate duty mine.
I sabotage myself with guilt.
This heinous, hideous, heart-racked crime.

I will not compromise my soul.
I will not take that path.
It's likely that I'll never know.
P'rhaps not least until I go.
And so my penance if needs be.
A lifelong fast until I'm free.

UNSEEN HANDS

'Focus on the happy times,' they said consolingly.
Inwardly I winced.
Don't they know the happy times
means opening up the gates of grief
because
the happy times
to me
means
we.

I trawl my mind for other times
where sorrow cannot see
But I squirm; and wriggle; and prevaricate.
And keep closed those gates; then slide again
to nothingness
where it's safe and quiet and hassle free.
A hidden oasis, where quite alone I can
think and feel
in semblance of some calm.

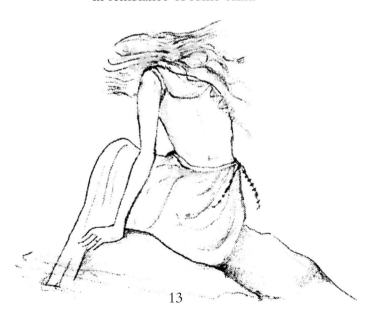

TWO INTO ONE

It's the little things that count, you know.
That something smile, that tickly touch.
And inch by inch you feel the glow;
and you know for sure, it's more than much.

'The other half'. You match so well.
Each part begets the whole.
Those nothing things we each can tell.
And the blossoming of heart and soul.

They say two into one just cannot go.
But what a fib that is.
When two souls blend, it's surely so.
Two into one just is!

DOWNHILL RUN

The slope looked so inviting. We HAD to try, could not resist
the powdery snow of the downhill piste.

We boldly ventured, heads bent low, pushing hard on bended
    knee.
'Wheee, down we go,' we yelled in childlike glee.
Willie, flying low, whizzed, of course, past little me.

I lagged behind but made with care to our allotted goal
where, to my surprise, what did I see,
my hero wrapped around a tree.
He'd landed there, of course – tee hee – turning back to look
    for me.
But undaunted up he got and dusted off.
So we joined at waist and glided short to final stop exactly on
our chosen space in the powdery snow of the downhill piste.

STAY! TINKER, STAY!

'Stay!
Tinker, stay!'
Obediently, Tinker sits at water's edge and watches.
Watches William as he pushes out to sea.
'Without me.'
Head lowered upon his paws,
stomach pressed against pebbles warm,
through velvet view
steadfast,
true,
he stares into the bluey calm.

The boat moves off with gentle glee.
'Without me …' A low growl returns the taunt, then
with bounding leap he's in the sea!
Swimming. Swimming with fervour bright,
keeping both in velvet sight.
With thud the bow is reached and,
swimming round,
with heave and hove
he's in the boat
safe and sound,
soaking wet
but seaward bound.
With William.

TREES

William and I love trees.
More than most, I guess.
We love the magic of a tree.
It gets right to the heart of us.
Sit quite still with empty mind
and you'll almost hear its mighty pulse.

Will and I love trees.
We run our hands along gnarled chests
in grossest human intimacy.
We talk with trees.
We sit with them.
We lounge against their mighty feet.

And somehow – undefinably –
We're snugly lost in a thousand dreams,
a thousand lifetimes.
For a brief short spell in a busy day.
William and me.

17

THE DRAGONFLY

A dragonfly alighted on my hand one day.
The merest tickle as it touched my skin.
sent ripples scurrying from hand to head.
From touch to brain.

And I gazed entranced, breath held as it led
my eye 'cross myriad dreams through translucent wings
as I paused awhile,
its teasing touch widening my watching smile.
And I was thrilled it shared something of itself.

It whirred from sight 'mong rustling reeds
and took a wealth so easily missed when we look
but fail to see.

A little glimpse, so beautiful, that fills so many human needs.
A silent interchange, words redundant.
Just quivering beauty
and human comfort.
All from one tiny dragonfly on a summer's day.
That time it flew along my way.

18

I CRIED AGAIN

I cried today. I cried again.
Great shaking gulping gasps.
Called out his name.
Dear God. Don't let this separation last.
      This dreadful pain.
      This lifelong fast.
I don't know what I'm doing here.
Waste of space when he's not near.

ANGEL FEATHER

Today this little angel feather
gently wafted to my feet.
It brings meaning of significance to the finder.
And now it's mine for me to keep.

Where it came from no one knows.
From realms unseen perhaps.
It carries many blessings
and a truer sense of self imparts.
So watch out for little angel wings.
They look like feathers.
Stoop low and pick one up.
Ignore the stares and whisperings.
You'll be surprised at what your little angel feather
      to you
      in secret
      brings.

MR LAIDBACK

Mr Laidback. What's in a name?
Just look at him.
Take a stroll down Laidback Lane.
He looks as if he's just
we-l-l, I don't know what.
Sleeves rolled up, track top lost.
Baggy jogs,
wearing socks?
And yet – that smile
says such a lot.
So even tempered.
for aye the same.
My Mr Laddie Laidback.
Down Laidback memory lane.

WAITING BOAT

The boat bobbed as it always did,
patiently waiting for its hand,
unaware that it was gone.
The hand grown close; boyhood long;
       grown close as one.
Familiar hand on tiller; a touch close known.

Journeying across the open seas,
charting waters with an ease
       grown since boyhood.
Man and boat. Boat and man.

Soon the waiting boat will sense an alien touch.
A different hand its tiller take.
Perhaps a different way to scour the seas.
And a different view will make.

The boat bobs and waits.
       Water laps its bows
preparing the small craft for its first trip
       without the hand
       it knows so well.

AND SO WE CHOOSE

There in the warm ocean in knee-high surf we bathed.
There on golden sands we lolled and lay.
What we've had we cannot lose, no one can ever take.
And so we journey; and so we choose which track to make
as we travel on our way through daily grind and daily play.
        And so we grow;
        and so we love;
        and so we mate.
And, having chosen, that we cannot lose;
and it's ours to keep and ours to take
        to memory's mine,
        ne'er to forsake.

THE BIKE

'What do you think of this?' he asked
     as I bent towards the stove.

'Yes dear, its beautiful,' I sighed,
     eyes glued to food roasting inside.

Imagine my surprise when I looked up.

Egad, what's this! A shining steed
behind my skirts. Oh my! Mr Meades!

     Some say I spoilt him.
       But what a lad.
     That beaming smile.
       I can't be sad.

SPENT REALITY

The soft strumming stirred my mind
as I watched long fingers, supple, strong
move eloquently along the struts
to make the sounds of a lilting song
that carried balm to heal and calm.

The gentle lilt, in wave-like flow
evoked a time, now part a dream.
A spent reality: that somehow seems
transformed as thought.
And each new thought, in reciprocity, currency gains,
transmigrating, changing form.
'til born again in new found shape
returns anew the spirit's song.
A legacy for you and me to carry
with us
all life long.

SKATING

Boots on, I sallied forth.
Grave error.
William, poised expectantly, waited
for the inevitable as I whipped and whirred
'cross polished ice.

In serious mode I did a turn.
Following soft behind my tail, I sensed his mirth.
The infectious chuckle caught my ear. And that was it!
Giggles grew to wobbles as the ice loomed close and white.
Careering round in mirth-held grip, the waiting ground embraced
my slip as I spun dizzily down in spiral dip
to the sound of Willie's laughter, deep and rich.

I whizzed and spun to his laughing tune, control deserted;
and all too soon I was in some void, tossed and turned
like small child's toy
'til lifted up by strong, brown hands.

I snuggled in as we skated off.
Naught could hide my iced, white bum,
but my prize I'd won;
a serious snuggle in Willie's arms;
and I was content in my icy world of merriment.

MY BED

My bed. Aha, my bed.
My comforter. My friend.
I snuggle in and tuck me tight
and drift in warmth through bleakest night.
I smell the taste of William's skin.
I close my eyes. I drink him in:
and float and dream and fantasise
of balmy days and sun-kissed skies.
And I'm gone into another world
of peace and love and blessedness;
where healing comes from wondrous Source:
And I awaken with a new-found force
                    to fill the day.
                        Again.

ENTRANCED

One summer's eve
I watched a butterfly gently glide upon a leaf
It lingered long,
savouring its chosen patch
lest in a trice all should be gone.

With breath 'pon breath
and beat 'pon beat,
the two, in rhythmic motion rare
there swayed in the gentlest breeze
       oblivious of all care.

In fascination hushed, I watched the pair
swaying gently; swaying there.
A little glimpse of Nature's world
and my sleeping sensibilities uncurled.
Freed from the fetters of rational bind
I was dreamily transported to reality
       of a different kind.

       Such a tiny picture.
       Such a fleeting glimpse.
That hovering butterfly and its chosen patch
       wedded in some timeless bliss.

Intriguing thought. Amazing sight.
Timeless perfection on a summer's night.
My curious mind, seeped in the sight,
tasted existence of a new-found kind.
       And I was entranced.
       Hooked,
by Nature's sensuous, rhythmic dance.

SWIMMING

Swimming side by side.
      Floating.
      Holding.
Surfing waves on coming tide.
Bathed by Caribbean blue.
We lapped it up.
In ice-cold waves
off Eastbourne beach
great breakers brought us to our knees.
And we laughed; and caught our breath
and shivered in the growing breeze.

In pools and lakes and little ponds
we swam and frolicked,
forgetting long the time-marked day.
      That was our way.
Splashing. Lazing. Floating. Swimming.
      Working hard but also making
      time to play.
And am I glad we went that way.

ABSENT

It feels really weird that William isn't here.
He is; and yet he's not.
His smiling picture keeps him near
but it's just an image that I've got
to touch and hold and chat to.
I cannot truly hold him
and I miss profound his great big arms around my tiny frame.
       It's weird
       It's horrid
       And I do not like this awful part of Life's
       little testing game.

THE SEA, THE SUN

The sea, the sun, the azure sky
and sweet William by my side.
We lived the dream. We played the game.
We rode our hopes, our spirits high.
And though my life won't be the same
      I dwell in memories fond
      in bittersweet refrain.
           And I live
           and live
           and live
           my time
        with William once again.

OARSMEN

Muscled frames heave as blades dip and lift.
The crew, as one, pull and skim, scything through the water,
focused for the win.
Heads forward, bodies bent, they heave and stretch and pull;
muscles pumping, foreheads, backs,
glistening with pumped-out sweat.

Iron will drives them on towards their goal;
as, in rhythmic tune, they dip, lift and hold.
Beautiful sight, rippling muscles at their best.
Effort-filled.
Propelled by will to race and win.
Contract. Relax.
Contract. Relax.
Bulge and flatten.
Pump.
Release.
Cutting through water with determined ease.
Pushing their craft through sliced-out path,
trailing white like unfurling flag
as they leave behind opponents tired,
disappearing from their sight.
Oarsmen primed, fighting fit for their sporting fight.

Oh, my William, my muscled man,
striving, pulling, to win the race
with your little clan
of mates.

WITHOUT INTENT

'I've eaten William's ashes.'
The words slid out like silvered fish.
And the lapping water, percussion-crashed between wet rocks,
echoed the words through swirling mist.
'I've eaten William's ashes.'
My brother's utterance honed missile-like home,
cutting clear the wet-wave crashes
to fall upon my listless ear
and share a truth not yet known.

I tapped my toe 'pon squelchy sand.
I felt his gaze as he squeezed my hand.
'I know,' I said and looked away,
' 'cause I've just done the same.'

My voice confessional caught his breath.
And he softly spake my name.

We sat awhile, poised and silent, musing both
upon the disapproved of deed;
while listening waves poised for retreat
lapped consolingly at our feet.
And we felt good.
Smug.

We laughed aloud. We splashed and jigged.
We'd done the deed not many would.
The waves awaiting at our feet
in rhythmic motion 'gan retreat.
Back to the sea.
To William,
with news well sent
of the deed we did without intent.

NIGHT'S STILLNESS

Night's stillness waits and watches,
Night's stillness cloaks and comforts.
Night's stillness speaks in whispers
Night's stillness soothes my troubled soul.

Why do we seek this still, still quiet
What are we listening for and why
What primordial urge compels us
to attend so closely to the quiet still
of the night ?

We all do it.
Even tiny babies do it.
We listen to the stillness.
And strain for some small cue.
And when we're troubled, stressed or sore.
We seem to do it all the more.

Strange phenomenon.
Seems primal. Psyche deep.
Way, way back in human mind
this listening, straining
to the quiet of the night.
What DO we seek ?

How do we know there's something there,
Tidgy, out of reach.
Night seems to know.
Its quiet watchfulness
suggests it's so

Yet steadfastly its secret keeps.
And so we listen and so we strain.
Far into the night
'til sunrise comes again.

EARTH MUSIC

Scurrying clouds skip across the sky.
fluffy white-tinged pink.
Scurrying onwards, 'cross canopy light
as birds soar and dip; then disappear from sight.
Aching neck drops head among green blades perfumed
and a mirrored scurrying comes to view.
A teeming microcosm greets the eye
and Earth, with low contented sigh,
murmurs so soft, 'tis scarcely heard;
but 'tis there for the discerning ear.
Prone body feels the tiny strummings and drummings
as Earth's music seeps the bones.
Senses drift in mute delight.
      Message received.
      Tacit, bright.
Soon my world will turn aright.
The long, dark tunnel's receding back into the night
      where it belongs
      and human soul's not meant to go.
      I sense the moment.
      The time is right.
      Gigantum task.
      I must let go.

MAKES YOU THINK

The squirrel scampered up the trunk
and at the very apex, stopped;
stared round; then, with descending rapidity,
    silently touched ground.
No sooner done than it was off into the mist
    Security.
Not much different from you and me
when, in our vulnerability
we duck and dive; and shift our scene;
    to hide.

Tall trees, like watching sentinels,
witnessed thus this spectacle;
and myriad stars began their dance out of sight
behind the dawn; behind the light.
Sight. Light. Hidden. Seen.
Repeating theme.
Nature. Human psyche.
Some mysterious link.
Makes you think.

LONGING

Why is it on a sunny day
the plane drones overhead?
Stirs my mind; evocative;
so much so I would be dead.

Oh, for a mind anaesthetised.
One clear, long stretch of emptiness.
One vast void where I can simply be.
And cradle in beatific state cocooned;
      the essenced me.
      This limbo state goes on too long.
      It wearies, tires, saps the strength;
      usurps my very core-life song.
I need to sing, to dance again;
to laugh and live my essence plain
      the way I'm meant to be.
It's such a long, long haul to make.
      Alone
      A solitary half.
      A part.
Without my mate to beat my heart.

WHOPPER

'It's a whopper!' the shout went out.
    And I followed crowd
       to have my 'see'.
And there they were, fish and he;
giants both, bonded by the sea.
They posed together, fish and man
until back it went; and off it swam
into its watery home, the foaming deep.
And I felt proud; and good;
Man and Nature sharing battled feat
in kind of cosmic brotherhood.

THE POND

There's a peaceful pond where anglers go.
It's near gnarled trees and bleating sheep.
Insects land, and stay, and rest
in its little world of blessedness.
　　　　How quiet.
　　　　How still.
This peaceful pond; green fringed and full of
　　　　little fish
is one of Nature's habitats; where lazy mullet miss
　　　　the bait
and damselflies flit in silent rainbow hues across
　　　　their mighty lake.
This peaceful pond by forest dark catches evening light from
sunbeams bright as they dance across its watery ways,
　　　　heralding thus approaching dusk
　　　　as it closes down another day.

Tall reeds wave their flag-borne tips;
　　　　and water ripples in reply.
　　　　And zephyr wind takes up the cue;
　　　　and lesser spotted woodpecker, sweeping low
　　　　'cross Mallard's back, displays for all, its splendid hues.

As dusk draws near the little pond changes gear
as it gently shuts for sleep.
Floating creatures drift through reeds
and, drifting, make their way
　　　　to rest.
　　　　To dream.
Until, like us, thus refreshed,
　　　　they wake
as dawn draws them out,
　　　　another day to take.

EMPTY SHELL

It once meant so much,
this beautiful home he's left behind.
Now it's just an empty shell.
Lost its touch.
And however much I try, motivation passes by.
It's somehow grown quite sad – a shadow of its former self
A house without a mind.

A house without a mind. No spark. No life.
Just sits and waits save in robotic motion when it does a bit.
No give or take.
The heat comes on. Switches click.
Doors open. Windows stick.
Water flows and stops.
It all seems jaded, faded, like a drooping, wilting flower
visibly dying by the hour.

The clock ticks on like Sergeant Plod.
Tick – Tock – Tick – Tock,
echoing through the empty rooms.
So clean. So neat. No gardening hands or muddy feet to mar
this pristine tomb.
It almost seems our lovely home is living sadly on its own
and quietly pining to return
to the home it used to be.

HOW DO I LOVE THEE?

I love thee as the morning mist
that glistens o'er the grass.
I love thee as the evening sun
that bathes the earth when day is passed.
I love thee as the stars above
that light the darkest night.
I love thee as the ocean deep
with all its power and might.
Through every sense,
with every pulse beat strong,
though only lent to me 'tis true,
my love is yours the whole life long.

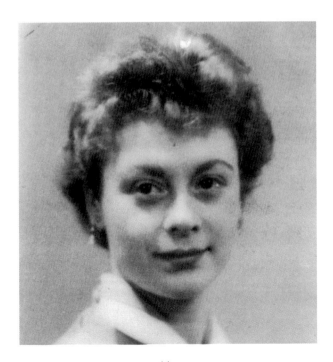

DOWN IN KENT

There's a little corner down in Kent.
A haven where the crippled ship can call.
It's somewhat secret; a private place.
It pulses with an unseen strength
that permeates the very air and lifts the weary resting there.
It's quietly busy with purpose strong.
        And all day long
        soft shadows flitter by
        alert for e'en the merest cry
        for help.
Like clockwork ghosts administering, the soft shadows guide
        and give and help and heal
        their human cargo vulnerable.
The church bell calls to prayer those waiting to be summoned there.
        And in the peace and quiet air
        bodies heal and souls repair.
Perhaps we sip sweet medicine divine
as in that place our trust we find.
In that little corner down in Kent.

CLANDESTINE STEALTH

Her sun returned one day without expect.
A shining ball of nectared bliss.
And it came in human form, unasked,
with clandestine stealth so eas' to miss.
The felt knowing seared: and sent
that fated feeling as if meant.

A sideways glance through lowered lash
swept o'er the profile, limbs and back.
Little echoes of William came.
Much like him – yet not the same.

The engine purred. The ride was smooth.
And, destination reached, she felt the glow
as she nestled snug into the seat,
savouring soft the clandestine treat.

Whate'er the motive of intent by chanced design,
it clearly meant a door ajar.
And through the crack there glimmered hope.
        Out there.
        A hope not far.
        The warmth was back.

RESPITE

The water swirls, white foam turned pink;
And I wallow in the liquid's scent,
recuperating from the bumps and strains
    and buffeting of daily grind.

Wallowing, dreaming, floating away
things from my mind in the soft white foam turned pink.
    Mind suspended.
    Feel.
    Don't think.

The bubbles swirl and drift away
    and I'm pink and on my feet
    as fluffy towel comes into play.
Then I'm back again for serious think
    of what's in store
    for coming day.

PRECISE THE TIME

Each morning at precise the time I awoke.
What woke me thus I could not tell.
Perhaps in sleep the moment I re-lived
      to take and keep,
remembering the death that went so well.
Some solace perhaps made me awake.
And I reflect the way it was
that early morn one year ago

Waking, the birds shared their song.
Each morn, through sleep-filled lids I looked.
      He was not there.
      My man had gone.
      His side empty,
      cold; and bare.
      He was not there.

Each morning, at precise the time,
      psyche primed,
      I awoke.
      And wept
      'til tear-filled eyes 'came screwed-up slits.
And I could weep no more.

So long ago; and yet so near.
      – a lifelong year
      – now just a dream
      – with thoughts still dear.

THE WHEEL TURNS

The wheel turns
and in turning
meets the new,
throws off the old.
Leaves indentations for all to see
'til Time, eradicator supreme
erases same, as if to say,
'Now let things be,
the past has gone.
It's had its time
and now its mine
to weave and spin
in tapestry divine.'

SURRENDER

Will I ever love again?
Could I ever love again
with like passion deep and strong
and true; and build another life anew?

Which might win, known rapture strong; or
the cutting cruelty of the pain
that seems to linger on and on?

More lucid moments meet my mind.
    And
    I suspect
    I feel
    I think
    I find
as I surrender to the Greater Will
the chance when given
that might be mine.

GOD LISTENS

The sun came up today.
Again.
How can the world remain the same when mine
has crumbled into pain.
I strain to see a sign outside that empathises soft,
articulates with how I feel
and shares this harrowing sense of loss.

Is that a cry among the trees?
A teardrop on that leaf?
Is that a darkening cloud that hovers o'er the summer
scene waiting to destroy the same,
a harbinger of loss and pain?

I turn away, and upon my bed I lie
in numb suspension cold.
Black cloud grows and comes indoors
and I tremble at its touch.
Then, with stunning force the sun streams in.
Black cloud dissipates 'mid snarling sighs.
And I know, deep down, despite my pain,
God listens to our cries.

THE THORNS

At daybreak whilst upon my bed,
eyes wide open, quite awake,
a crucifix flew to my head; and I watched
it there in 3D shape transfixed.
The Crucified with crown of thorns was hanging nailed.
    So passive.
    Pensive.
    So forlorn.
My heart went out; but empathy evoked was soon
    to dismay born.
For as I watched, a spiky, digging, dark barbed wire
was coiling round the Christ-hung form.
    Turning.
    Twisting.
    From toe to top.
    Ripping.
    Cutting.
    Refused to stop.
Piercing the Christ-flesh, relentless so.

I gasped and grimaced at each turn.
And felt the pain as though my own.
My spirit wept. He looked so passive. So forlorn.
But as I reached to help him down
    He suddenly was gone.
    And in His place
    upon my head
A very puzzled human frown.

Footnote: In hospital during painful recuperation after surgery.

BACK TO ROOTS

The distant train called out as it sped through frosty morn
whilst world awaited day's new birth.
And nothing stirred. Human sound, not yet born
Missed my purpose as I slipped with resolution firm to my
    secret assignation.

The door shut soft. The gate, by habit, clicked.
And I glanced at windows curtained drawn
as down the lane in silent step
I toed it past the sleeping curr.
Then walked, mind set,
to keep my rendezvous as sworn.

The stars had gone when uphill path began to stir
and bird trill sang awake.
Up and up on downland track my muscles pumped,
pulling assignation near.
Drawing in the slack.

Below, a world of mist through which peered
Sneaky, mocking little lights.
And I spat at them with venom blast, heaving for the promised
    fight.
On I strode; and on and on oe'r dew wet blankets green
where sweethearts kissed in Spring.
And I knew my heart still lingered there as I walked in
    'membered bliss.

At length the very spot came near.
The spot, which, long ago I held most dear.
And there It hovered – that demon, Pain.
      Smirking.
      Gloating
on hallowed ground.
On our very own terrain.

So powerful the taunt. So meticulous its mark.
I shook and bawled and bellowed as the tears flowed fast and hot;
And I beat the air with clenched fists white.
With legs astride I beat and smote that smirking sop
with all my mustered might.

My furry friends, in startled mode fled
to safety holes and cosy nests,
tucking in their soft-fur heads
away from all 'this human mess'.
Some while I stood astride that turf and vent
my angst in holler loud
whilst Nature watched and waited;
and little creatures cowed.
Then, from out nowhere, the fairest wind whispered
through the Downland air.
In gossamer hold it took up my cries out to the waiting sea
there to die in watery dissipation.

I'd kept my assignation.
Confronted Pain and sent it off.
I'd left my card for all to know
that ne'er again in this life form
would forces such attack this soul,
On its way to source where surely it first
      came from.

LITTLE TENT

I made a little tent
where no nurse could see me cry.
And I sobbed into the silent night
why did my William have to die?
To me it doesn't seem quite right
for him to go away.
He wouldn't leave by choice, I know,
he'd always choose to stay.
I wonder WHY he had to go?
I hope he's happy wherever so.
If unhappiness there has to be,
I hope it stays right here with me.
I'm not yet good enough to be set free.

Footnote: The loss, separation and trauma of surgery were almost unbearable.

THE COPSE

Cast shadows beneath dappled canopy.
The copse looks inviting,
beckoning the curious 'cross green-decked floor.

The little copse stands apart from human strife
and grows there, undisturbed, sheltering its growing life.
No human voice disturbs its still.
No raucous laughter or shrill tones
puncture the quiet air of this peaceful place,
here in this little copse.
A living testament of God's good grace.

LAUGHTER

Daisy's little face lit up. She beamed. It filled the room.
Elliot caught it. Bounced it off. And soon we were giggling.
And our giggling turned to quake-like quivering.
Then great guffaws filled the air as we rolled about
   laughing there.

What made us laugh so we didn't know,
except that when we'd finally settled down
with aching ribs and stern-like frowns
trying to be serious,
Daisy chuckled; and Elio and Duncan looked and saw
that Uncle Bry was 'peering down'.

Soon it dawned upon us four that we held in hand
forever more 'the jewel in the crown'.
And that if we ever felt a little down, we'd just think
of Uncle Bry when he played about and made us laugh
'til our ribs ached and we rolled around.

SALAD DAYS

'Aah. Salad days.'
Will's favourite phrase
as we cheered the gees down Plumpton way
or fished the rock pools 'neath the Head
      for darting prawns for tea.

The salad days. Our beacon bright
as we tramped the Downs for lush, pink
mushrooms skulking out of sight.
Or pushed great shrimp nets in waist-high wet
      'neath smiling moon for half the night.

The salad days. Contentment filled.
Little picnics 'twixt soft Sussex hills.
And endless jokes and bantering
'til tiny offspring fell about, mirth-drunk
      and tottering.

We have to smile and carry on.
We cannot waste such well spent fun.
So the painful loss that cuts us deep
must needs give way to the gifts
      we're given to share and keep.

GLOWING LIGHT

One year ago the life I knew and loved was, without warning, gone.
Since then I've travelled on.
Alone.
I've tried to comprehend the whys and wherefores.
But answers have I none.

The wise, the learned, spiritually astute; the young, the old; the meek, the bold.
I've searched them out; scoured my world.
But whys and wherefores still evade.
Not known.
Not yet.
I have to travel on.
I have to learn to wait.

Yet through the solitude, through the pain, a special light glows bright.
From There.
Way, way, way out there.
Glows bright from other Place, deep psyche felt.
Sent with care.
From some other where.

Strange mysteries have touched my soul; have whispered songs I did not know.
And people came – on wing and prayer.
Materialised from where?
Came and met.
Some stayed.
Some went.
All as if sent.

And Nature's healing benevolence – unasked help –
provided succour; blest this scruffy, insignificant part of human-ness.
And I am humbled.
Contrite.
Feel oh, so small
at my micro part in this greater whole.

THE GARDEN

Here in sheltered garden fair
a mini world teems with life
as insects scurry here and there
and larger creatures stalk the night.

Cruelty haunts this idyllic scene,
Large eats small: and small, sent scurrying
disappear down cavernous cracks
to who knows where?
They don't come back.

And the larger creatures poke and stare
at the empty space that once was packed
with tasty little morsel snacks.

For what all this? Such mindless motion
in chain-held grip.
These little lives, the microchips of Earth's surmise
are spent too quick
for mortal mind to accommodate.

So what of us - we teeming lot?
We scurry, stalk; and hunt and plot
to injure, hurt, debase or lower
those offenders of our ego's pride.
Then hatch great schemes, politician-like, to cover
o'er what really is so gross we needs must hide.

So in our garden world, what shelter do we find?
It too teems with life. It too holds strife
and the vulnerable get left behind.
Something grander than ourselves
needs must succour give
lest we too fall into cracks
and lose life's grip.
          The will to live.

MEN OF STEEL

He vaulted steel gate
in fluid flight,
reminiscent of days gone by
when knights in armour displayed
and won fair maiden's hand.
Gallant and fine, eager, bright.
My modern, ardent, courageous knight.

One other so, a life ago, I knew and held.
Of milder steel but yet so fine.
A shining spur, valour gelled.
So gallant, true, and honour filled.

Reality ripples, running through aeons of time,
Primus born, now held beneath indefinite dust.
        Layered.
Layered beneath earth and crust.
Ashes of dead and dying,
realities surfacing in rippled kind,
keeping in motion the eternal mind.

Perpetual prompts of long-gone lives.
        The wheel turns
        Bodies die.
        Ashes fall
        and return as soul.
And so we're born; and so we go,
to return again
in some new form.

KISS OF THE SUN

The kiss of the sun upon my lips.
The whispering wind that trawls my hair.
Those unseen hands that lift me up.
I feel your presence everywhere

My bewildered senses overflow.
I'm in a world where's hard to know
what's real. What's true. And how very difficult
it is to let you go
when only yesterday, mid stream of love,
we laughed and hugged in that sunny place
that's suddenly a life ago.

Footnote: The place where William died.

WHIZZING ALONG

Whizzing along green leafy lanes on the battered old A.J.S.
hair flying, face stinging,
and Willie and me, crescendo singing.
Whizzing along on the A.J.S.
Carefree and happy, halcyon days.
Sun drenched and fruit filled
along leafy lanes
and meandering ways.

Soaked to the skin we'd race along lakeside routes,
cross purple moors to valleys rich and green.
And we'd wring our clothes, then dress again in
garments cold and wet
'mid drenching, driving rain
'til bike, protesting loud, would force us off to
push and pull, and heave and strain, still singing
songs until the sun would out again.

Then off we'd go, with a wheeeee and a whoosh,
whizzing along green leafy lanes
on the battered old A.J.S.

LITTLE DEMONS

The Devil's little demons may try to catch you out.
They wait, and hide and hover; then pounce
without announcement; and flout
the rules of healing to set you back again.
And soon you find you're drowning in that
dreadful sea of pain.

The Devil's little demons need keeping well at bay.
You've got to knock 'em sideways by whatever
and which way.
Keep strong and straight and resolute
and they'll wither and despair.
Build castles in the air.
Dig holes in earth so black.
Whatever else you do or dare,
shake those devilish demons off your back.

FROM A MILLION LIVES

From a million lives before,
    I came.
And in this one, am but a part,
A waking accumulation of some primeval past.

Insistent, these prehistoric things creep
    into my waking space
to nullify my mind of current thought
and cause the feeling part predominate.
    I try to shed this other self
to clear out mire – accumulated gain.
But still I am in part that which
then I was; and shall tomorrow be again.

LOVE DOES NOT DIE

Love does not die with the body.
      It lives for ever,
through incarnation after incarnation.
  Love is stronger than death.
      Not any dogmas,
      not any philosophy,
      creed or human grandiosity,
      not any great ideal,
nothing in this world,
nothing in the next
shall prevent those who love from
      the certainty
      of rejoining
      sometime,
      somewhere,
      somehow,
the soul they love.

NO TEARS TO CRY

The rain lashed long across the Downs,
battering low, and flattening, as it scythed
and cut the soft, undulating ground.
Wind abetted, whipping up in furious vent
its fearsome force without relent.
Cowering creatures, 'twixt tiny tufts of greenery tried to hide
their whimpering offspring from the maelstrom force
      of Nature's genocide.

I watched impassive the tumultuous scene,
windowed secure; warm and dry.
I listened to the young ones cry and shed no tear.
      I had no tears. My eyes had dried.
For hours I sat and watched and heard a world gone mad.
A happy, little mini world of scampering creatures, wheeling birds;
and crawling insects in chalk-speckled mounds of roots upturned.

      At last came still.
      Heartbeat quiet.
And bit by bit greenery began to twitch;
And nervous noses tweaked and sniffed.
And I felt glad their harrowing time was but short-lived.
      Unlike mine.
      But I could not cry with them.
      My tears had all run dry.
      I had no tears to cry.

THE FEEL-GOOD FACTOR

A spot of sun, that's all it takes
to set the ball a-rolling.
A bird that soars upon the wing.
A little smile. A gentle touch.
A baby's gurgle.
All these bring back life and hope.

It's the feel-good factor.
The bounce-back bit.
Can't keep it down 'gainst Nature's
stacked up goodies.
Persistent.
Pulsing. New-life packed.
The F.G.F.
It makes one rise against ogre hurts
and greedy grief
that feed upon the troubled soul.

A spot of sun
brings out our best.
And we're back again on our lifelong quest
for Source.

ASTRAL TRAVEL

She was running. Effortlessly. Fleet of foot.
            Amazing sight.
Bounding, running towards white light.
In rapturous joy she sped along beside green hedge
            verdant bright.
Arms a-stretch; streaming hair soft behind.
            And that joy.
            Ecstatic.
Seldom known by humankind.

As I watched I felt infused.
Separate, yet a part of it.
Who was she; and going where, this maid
who looked a lot like me.
            Running.
            Bounding.
            Joyfully.

An outstretched arm came into view.
            and as tips touched
I suddenly knew, before I'd even glanced ahead
that though I was here and in my bed
I was also there: and that girl was me.
            And, therefore,
            for that brief time
I was running, bounding: astral free
            to who knows where.
Is this perhaps, how souls repair?

66

GIANT AMONG MEN

'Once in a lifetime you may meet a giant among men; someone who has a charisma so powerful that you feel you can reach out and touch it. What is charisma? It is the ability to inspire, and it is at its most powerful when it is founded on serenity.'

Robert Frazer: *Notes for My Son*, 1977

Thank you William, my giant among men.

Ginny

67

PICTURE CREDITS